Codependency

A Simple Guide to Break Free from the
Codependent Cycle, Release Negative Self-Talk
and Start Creating Healthy Relationship

Bianca Sutton

Table of Contents

Introduction

R elationships are complicated and confusing. To make things even more complicated and confusing, we add our own personal style to each relationship. Some relationship difficulties include challenges with communication, self-esteem, honesty, and trust. One term commonly used in describing relationships is codependency. Codependency may be defined as a person having an excessive emotional need to be involved or partnered with someone else for support and control. Codependency is a destructive pattern that limits the person's life and relationships. Andrew Potterfield explains codependence in his book, "The Lifelong Activist". He says, "Codependence refers to a form of learned behavior that involves placing the needs of another person ahead of your own. This can lead to depression when you're unable to meet other people's needs, resentment when you're forced to give up your happiness for someone else's and an overwhelming sense of powerlessness when you feel trapped in a relationship.

Codependency (or codependency) also describe a relationship with an addict or abusive person. It is also called "relationship addiction." The term was coined by the co-founders of Alcoholics Anonymous (AA) in the 1930s and is now used in social work, psychiatry, and substance abuse recovery. Co-dependents often deny that their behavior problems have anything to do with another person; they tend to blame themselves for all their problems. They usually feel they must take complete responsibility for everyone and everything.

Co-dependents may have been raised by parents with a mental health disorder, who were unemployed or underemployed, or were emotionally unavailable or by parents who had alcohol or drug problems, who were physically cruel to them, or who never related to them at all. Co-dependents tend to have a great need for control driven by low self-esteem; however, they do not see themselves as having it. Co-dependents thrive on relationships with other people and will do almost anything to avoid being alone. Their love is dependent upon another person's performance. They are very seldom physically violent but are frequently verbally and emotionally violent toward themselves and/or others.

Co-dependents are characterized by a fear of abandonment. When in relationships, they put their own needs last or not at all; however, when left alone, they feel abandoned, even though they may have been the party that ended the relationship.

When confronted, a co-dependent will use denial, rationalization (make excuses), minimization, and blame-shifting (blaming others for their feelings or problems). They fail to assume responsibility for their own thoughts and behaviors. They frequently feel that they do not have what it takes to be loved or to love others. Their self-esteem is usually very low; they have difficulty making decisions and find it difficult to trust themselves. They are also very concerned with other people's opinions.

Co-dependents tend to be insecure and have difficulty making decisions on their own. They fear abandonment and cling to others, trying to control them to feel safe. Their relationships tend to be very intense but short-lived. In their relationships, co-dependents often play the role of rescuer or caretaker (the person who takes responsibility for everyone's feelings and problems). They may feel that they can fix the problems of the other person. They may focus on another person's strengths and ignore or minimize their weaknesses. Co-dependents need people around them all the time to feel safe and secure. Because they have difficulty being alone, they tend to fill every waking moment with activity, partly to avoid reflecting on themselves or feeling insecure about being alone. Co-dependents tend to have few, if any, close friends.

Co-dependents also tend to have problems with low self-esteem, exaggerated or inappropriate guilt, and difficulty making decisions. Many co-dependents are "people-pleasers." They try to get others to like and admire. They are sometimes called "superficial" friends because they appear emotionally healthy on the outside. Other people are often unaware of the real problems of co-dependents.

Like an alcoholic, a co-dependent's personality is dependent on mood-altering behavior to reduce stress and anxiety. Their behavior is not a rational response to stress but an attempt to steady their internal emotional system. They will frequently look for love and acceptance from others, but they don't seem able to give love themselves. They often have poor self-concepts and low self-esteem; they feel that they are bad or undeserving. They usually feel bored and empty; they may also be depressed, anxious, or scared.

They tend to criticize themselves. They are usually in a negative emotional state. Co-dependents are usually preoccupied with worry and anxiety due to their fear of abandonment. This causes them to be emotionally needy, dependent on other people for their emotional well-being and stability. They usually lack the capacity to be alone without feeling lonely. Their self-esteem is usually dependent on the emotions of others, so that when someone they relate to does not respond to them, they feel rejected and abandoned. They are easily hurt and often become victims.

Because co-dependents tend to focus on pleasing others (rather than themselves) and neglect their own needs, they do not make good friends or partners. They are afraid that if others get to know the really them, they will not be liked or loved. They usually don't trust themselves. They don't think they have anything of value to offer. Because of their sense of powerlessness, co-dependents often seek out people who have a great deal of personal power and charisma. They may be attracted to an individual who is emotionally unavailable. They often marry individuals who have a borderline personality.

The most significant relationship in every person's life is the relationship with their parents. People repeat the emotional and behavioral patterns established in childhood. The way your parents treated you greatly determines the quality of your relationships as an adult and how you treat others.

In order to survive, children (even infants) need to attach themselves to one or both parents; otherwise, they will not survive emotionally or physically.

Notes

Chapter 1:
What is Codependency

C o-dependency can be described as an addiction to another person, even if that person is addicted to or dependent on something else. It is a pathological relationship whereby the codependent acts in dysfunctional ways but doesn't realize it. Codependents are often addicts. Sometimes the "codependent" person is actually a child of an addict and is now acting out the addictive behaviors of the parent.

Child-adult "codependency" occurs when a child's emotional needs are met by an adult. That adult is not a parent or guardian and this imbalance of power causes the child emotional distress or trauma that is greater than typical childhood distress. A child dependent upon a teacher, minister, coach, adult relative or neighbor for care and nurturing will suffer trauma and dysfunction greater than that of a normal child.

Co-dependents are people who contribute to their own unhappiness by being overly helpful and selfless toward others, at the expense of their desires and needs. Even though they may be well-intended, co-dependents often enable others' bad behavior and hurt themselves in the process. Also known as "fixers", people with co-dependent tendencies often develop several specific characteristics and compulsions.

Codependency can give rise to several dysfunctional behaviors which can seriously harm the relationship of the victim and their abuser. A codependent relationship is essentially an abusive relationship where the abuser is in denial about their own abusive behavior. The abuser will always want to shift the blame to the codependent for any problems. If a partner tries to comfort them and tell them that everything is going to be all right, this will often be met with anger and accusations of being patronizing, condescending or controlling.

This dysfunctional relationship can lead to feelings of disappointment, hurt, anger and outrage. The victim may feel they are being emotionally abused by their partner; however, they are usually denied access to their partner's emotions. They can also feel a sense of frustration due to the fact that their abusive partner cannot be helped. It is generally easier to walk away from an abusive relationship than to get someone else to change, which is why people with codependent tendencies often find themselves in relationships where they are abused.

Codependents can be of any age, race or financial status. They are often found in abusive situations, whether as the abuser or the abused. They may also indulge in other addictive behaviors including spending, eating disorders, and overwork. The majority of co-dependents are women with low self-esteem who were raised by addicted parents (often called ACOAs: Adult Children of Alcoholics).

For them, it's a matter of survival. Their need to take care of their co-dependent partner is so overpowering that they are willing to sacrifice their own needs and happiness just to keep the relationship intact.

They are found in all walks of life. They are usually passive people who have difficulty expressing anger and don't respond well to stress. They are very sensitive to other people's and desires. This makes them the last person anyone would assume is having an affair or acting inappropriately.

Co-dependents usually have no idea that they exhibit codependent behavior until someone tells them they are doing so (usually a therapist). The co-dependent will do anything for their partner because they are either afraid or unable to set boundaries, enforce limits, or exert self-control. They have an unshakeable feeling of love for the person who takes advantage of them. They want to preserve the relationship at all costs.

The co-dependent person will blame others and make excuses for their loved one. They will not take responsibility for themselves because they need to preserve the relationship. This is called denial.

Another behavioral trait of codependents is that they tend to be highly responsible. They often step in and take over complete responsibility for tasks at home, work, or with friends and family. When someone else is unable or unwilling to do something, the codependent person will gladly take on that task. Because their loved ones are looking up to them, they believe it is their responsibility to make sure that everything gets done.

For codependents, the needs of others come before their own. To them, love is a feeling of "all about me" while a lack of love equals "all about you". They think that to be loved, they have to put their own feelings on hold and cater to the needs of the other person or people in their lives. They become so focused on the unhealthy relationship that they forget about their own needs.

Unlike other addictions, codependency is not about getting high. Instead, it's the need to be in control and fix things. The codependent person will usually feel anxious and/or guilty when faced with a problem or crisis they can't solve or control.

Another hallmark of codependency is the constant rescuing of one's partner at the expense of one's own feelings and needs (emotional care-taking). The codependent will get angry at their partner, but the anger is quickly turned back on themselves. They feel depressed and lonely because they have pushed people away and lost touch with their real selves.

It can be difficult for a co-dependent to admit to being in an unhealthy relationship. To change, they must first acknowledge their role in the relationship. Denial often prevents them from getting help. Indeed, co-dependents need a great deal of help recognizing that they are stuck in an unhealthy pattern of relating to others.

Many ACOAs have trouble setting boundaries with their co-dependent partner and encouraging them to stay in therapy. This is because the codependent person often makes excuses for their alcoholic spouse or other family member.

The partners or parents of those with an addiction are so focused on their spouse or family member that they're unable to set boundaries and enforce limits. They blame themselves when things go wrong and often take the blame for their loved one's addiction.

The codependent will do anything to avoid conflict and will put their partner's needs ahead of their own. They will rearrange their lives to accommodate the needs of their partner. In short, they are so focused on the relationship that they don't take care of themselves.

In order to have a healthy relationship, the co-dependent must learn how to set boundaries and enforce limits. They must accept themselves as someone separate from others and make choices based on what they need rather than what others want from them. To set boundaries, the co-dependent must first recognize that they are in an unhealthy and unsatisfying relationship. They may need to enter therapy to determine what expectations they have of their partner and how they can make changes in their own behavior.

Notes

Chapter 2:
Signs of Codependency

M ost of us have been raised with a fair share of codependent tendencies. They may have come from our parents,
or other significant authority figures. It could even be our own
natural reaction to certain situations. Either way, codependency
is not something we are born with; it is learned behavior. We may
not even recognize that we are codependent at first. Sometimes
we don't know there is a problem until someone points it out to
us.

Here are some signs to look for:

If someone has failed to meet your needs, and you constantly
achieve closure with the statement, "I will never do business with
that person," then you may have a codependent nature. If you
continue to have dealings with that person, you are setting yourself up for a disappointment because that person is not likely to
change for you.

It is better to learn from the experience and move on to someone
who will meet your needs rather than spend your life placing expectations upon people who ultimately lead you down the path of
being disappointed.

If your self-esteem depends on what other people think of you,
you are codependent. Unless our self-esteem comes from ourselves first, it can never be stable or strong. If you spend your life
seeking approval from other people, you are not free to disagree
with them. Those who care about you will sometimes have differ-
ing opinions, and your self-esteem shouldn't come crashing down
if they don't agree with your way of thinking.

If other people's success makes you feel bad about yourself, you are codependent. You need to see the beauty in their accomplishments without feeling that their success is taking away from yours. We all have different areas of success, and we shouldn't feel threatened if someone else is doing better than we are in another area.

If you are obligated to help other people, but they don't reciprocate your efforts, you are codependent. You need to learn how to say "no" in order to live out the balanced life that God wants for you. You can offer help when appropriate without allowing others to use you without consideration or gratitude.

If you feel you cannot function without the approval of others, you may be codependent. You need to learn to find your own self-worth and base your worth on what God says about you, instead of looking for another person's approval.

If you feel you have to change yourself to fit other people's desires or expectations, you are codependent. A spouse is not supposed to change who you are and how you believe; a spouse is supposed to love the person he or she married.

If your work or social life takes a backseat to taking care of your partner, you may be codependent. Since your marriage is a partnership, you need to have your interests and hobbies taken care of, as well. You should have the freedom to pursue your own passions without having to talk to your spouse about it first.

If you are preoccupied with controlling other people's behaviors or emotions, you may be codependent. You need to search for a balance between caring about what people think and not being so worried about them that you don't allow them to make their own decisions.

If you feel you have to control your partner in some way, you may be codependent. Partners are supposed to love each other and encourage each other's growth, not hinder it. You should be able to trust one another with your lives, without fearing the worst.

If you feel undeserving of any praise and would rather accept blame for the things that go wrong, you may be codependent. You must learn to accept the blame for your own actions. You cannot be responsible for everyone's needs and problems; you need to be responsible for your own.

If you feel that you are not good enough to make it in life without someone else's help, you are codependent. You should be able to stand on your own two feet without having to depend on someone else to succeed or survive.

If you find yourself doing things to help others, are not getting appreciation for it and are constantly "doing for others," but never for yourself, you may be codependent. You must find a balance between helping others and taking care of yourself. This doesn't mean you should take advantage of the people around you, but it does mean that you should be willing to give yourself time to relax.

If your self-worth relies upon how well your significant other is doing in life or business, you may be codependent. A person's success is his or her business, and it should not affect you.

If you feel compelled to do whatever someone else wants, and you find it difficult to say "no," you may be codependent. You need to learn to speak up for yourself and say what you feel or need without feeling guilty. Each person should make decisions based on their own needs and not on the whims of someone else.

If you feel like you constantly need to fix something broken, or help others through their crises, you may be codependent. You need to learn the difference between helping a friend in need and being responsible for everything that happens in their lives. You cannot be responsible for other people's problems, and you cannot change the world around you.

If someone close to you has a problem, and you sometimes feel like it is your own fault for not helping them through it, you may be co-dependent. You need to learn to let people take responsibility for what happens in their own lives. You need to learn to live your own life without allowing the bad choices of others to have an impact on you.

If you see yourself in these examples, you may be codependent. But what if you don't see yourself in them? Many times we are codependent, but we do not know it. Or sometimes, we are oblivious because it has become a natural part of who we are.

If any of the above examples sound like you, it is essential that you separate codependency from healthy caring and helping. Once you recognize there is a problem, only then can you begin to address it.

You can learn to set boundaries and limits. You can learn to say "no" when you need to, or how to ask for help when you feel that you need it.

But most of all, remember that you are not responsible for fixing anyone's life but your own. You cannot change anyone's behavior, and you cannot always make someone else happy. This is not your job; it is theirs. All that you have control over is yourself and how you react in a given situation.

Some of these signs are a wakeup call for you to changes things. It is not easy to break the chains of codependency, but it is possible. Believe in yourself and believe that it is possible for you. Many people have overcome codependency and will not let it rule their lives anymore.

One of the best tools for overcoming codependency is to talk to someone who knows how you feel. A counselor or therapist can give you practical support. They can help you learn to trust your own judgment and make good decisions without you second guessing yourself.

Chapter 3:
Advantages and Disadvantages of Codependency

A lthough many believe that codependency is a sign of a strong relationship, it can eventually take its toll on a couple's communication skills and ultimately the future of the relationship. This chapter will discuss the advantages and disadvantages of codependency in a couple's relationship.

Advantages of Codependency

1. People are able to spread their own goodwill toward others and develop more intense relationships. This advantage is very important for the development of relationships with others because people have a unique opportunity to really get to know each other and understand what most attracts them in their partners.

2. Most people can get rid of their complexes and stop being afraid of an independent existence. Sometimes it's easier just to be there for someone else, as you can forget about your own problems and even the problems of others. Using all the effort at hand to help someone else, you can forget about your problems and only pay attention to another person's.

3. The person maintains a happy relationship with another person by opening up and expressing their feelings. It is not easy to express your feelings and talk about the feelings.

It gives the feeling of being special for the person who is in a co-dependent relationship because co-dependents will do everything to show their love and care for their partner. It gives the feeling of being needed; this is very important because people need to feel special and needed by others.

4. Co-dependent people feel that they have a purpose in life because they are able to help people in need. Most of the time, the co-dependent will feel they are helping others, but without a doubt, it is the other person who is, in fact, helping by getting support and care from someone else.

5. The individual is able to develop better relationships with people in their social environment, as well as contribute positively to the community or society they live in. This is a very important advantage because people become more social and active members of their community.

6. Co-dependent individuals fulfill their desires for human companionship by becoming involved in a co-dependent relationship. They are also able to make others happy and satisfied because they give rather than take in their relationships.

Disadvantages of Codependency

1. The individual who is co-dependent with another person is likely to feel a sense of desperation when the other party does not react according to expectations. This disadvantage is very much related to the fact that people are, at some point, likely to try to control others for things to go the way they want.

2. People who become co-dependent with other people might realize that they have lost their individuality and start feeling like a part of a single unit with the other person. This disadvantage is closely related to the advantages because in some cases, if you are able to be there for someone else all the time, you forget about your own needs and wishes.

3. The co-dependent individual may experience physical and psychological symptoms such as feeling worthless, helpless, unhappy, and confused when the relationship is threatened with disconnection from their significant other. In most cases, people who are co-dependent with others are afraid of being alone and will do everything to prevent it.

4. Co-dependent people are likely to be unable to function successfully in society because they will control their own emotions, as well as their own relationships with others. It is a very common

thing for co-dependents to feel they have no control over their lives and that they depend on others entirely.

5. If the individual becomes dependent on alcohol or drugs to sustain the relationship, they are at risk of developing an addiction that could cause irreversible damage to their life and responsibilities.

6. The co-dependent individual is likely to experience a sense of loneliness once the relationship with the other person ends, or if the other person does not reciprocate positively. There is always the possibility that the co-dependent person will remain in a relationship with someone who may care for them or provide them with a sense of security.

7. The individual is at risk of developing post-traumatic stress disorder by experiencing rejection on a regular basis or by constantly putting pressure on themselves to fulfill the needs of their significant other.

8. The individual is at risk of feeling trapped because they will constantly need the significant others to be happy and complete. They also are likely to feel they cannot go anywhere without the approval of their significant other.

9. The individual may experience hopelessness and despair because they are not able to maintain positive relationships with others, while also maintaining a healthy emotional balance. Basically, there is a risk that the co-dependent person will become isolated and lost in their own social environment and reality.

10. By being dependent on another person for happiness, it is likely they will develop a sense of inadequacy that could affect their self-confidence in day-to-day life.

11. The co-dependent individual is at risk of developing feelings of resentment toward the person they are dependent upon. Codependency is often a one-way path where the people involved in the relationship are not willing to reciprocate with co-dependent behavior but rather demand more attention and care from their partner without giving any in return.

12. The co-dependent individual is at risk of developing an emotional bond with the person they are dependent upon, where they are in a position of powerlessness and constantly blame themselves for the other person's problems.

13. The co-dependent individual is at risk of developing a sense of low self-esteem due to their inability to cope with the consequences of being involved in a relationship that is not healthy nor equal.

14. The co-dependent individual is at risk of developing mental disorders such as anxiety and depression which are caused by the inability to cope with a relationship characterized by constant demands for attention.

15. The co-dependent individual is at risk of developing heart disease and high blood pressure due to the stress placed on the body from trying to keep a relationship intact.

16. The co-dependent individual is at risk of developing negative health behaviors such as exposing themselves to unsafe sexual activity or poor eating habits due to the need to please their significant other.

Codependency is a condition that occurs when one individual becomes dependent on another person for meeting their needs in life. The people involved in the relationship are most likely to be either family members or good friends. It is important to understand that codependency can occur in any type of relationship, and the conditions that arise from codependency vary depending on the level of intensity.

Notes

Chapter 3:
Types of Codependent Behavior

T here are a range of behaviors in codependency, and there are several types of behaviors and symptoms. What is codependency? Codependency is any behavior that helps a person cope with feelings he or she cannot address on his or her own. These feelings can be of sadness, anger, fear, anxiety, shame and other painful emotions. The feelings are often directed at the self and may include feelings of not being "good enough", or they may be directed at others and feel more like a need to be responsible for the other person. Codependent behavior is the way people cope with their own painful feelings or take care of other people.

There are major types of codependent behavior:

External control of self

Individuals who are externally controlled by others tend to be less assertive and are easily influenced by the opinions, choices and desires of those around them. Individuals who have unstable self-images may look outside themselves for guidance to feel accepted and validated. A codependent person will allow their life to be directed by another individual so long as they are receiving the approval from others that they lack inside.

This person will believe that others know better in all aspects of life. Codependency is usually formed out of an inability to separate from a parent or caregiver at a young age. As a result, the codependent will idealize this attachment figure and relate to other people based on how they fit their idealized image of the parent or caregiver.

Avoidant behavior

Someone who exhibits avoidant behavior is often very sensitive to rejection and has difficulty with relationships. They do not see how they push people away and keep them at a distance. They experience low self-esteem and shame about their past and present life.

A person exhibiting obsessive-compulsive disorder believes they are superior to others in some way or they need to be perfect in every way possible. They have a strong fear of being humiliated and will go to great lengths to avoid it.

Narcissistic behavior

People who are narcissistic do not see themselves as needing others. They have a sense of grandeur, where they believe they are special and therefore entitled to special treatment. They may be aggressive or angry in an attempt to hide inner feelings of shame or low self-esteem. They may be controlling to keep others dependent on them. This type of behavior is often caused by childhood trauma.

Egocentric behavior

It is normal to refer to oneself as or feel like you are the center of the universe. For people with egocentric behavior, it goes beyond this, and they have a difficult time seeing or acknowledging anyone else's feelings or needs. This type of behavior is sometimes caused by codependency, where the person feels responsible for someone else's emotions, making it hard for them to see anyone else's viewpoint or even another's needs and feelings. An example of this behavior is someone who interrupts conversations or doesn't listen while others are talking because they are focused on themselves.

Attention-seeking behavior

People with this type of behavior use codependent behaviors to attract attention from others. This is often caused by someone feeling that they are not experiencing unconditional love in childhood from their parents. They may be trying to prove how lovable they are through the way that other people treat them.

Narcissistic abuse

This type of abuse is usually intentionally hurtful and is often found in relationships that include a narcissist and codependent. A typical pattern of abuse includes periods of criticism, judgment, and disdain followed by brief remorse or increased attention from the narcissist. The source of the problem isn't the narcissist, but the codependent who is unable to set limits or boundaries, take responsibility for himself or herself, or recognize his or her part in creating a dynamic relationship. An example of this narcissistic abuse is when a partner with narcissistic behavior repeatedly calls his or her partner names in an attempt to degrade them, telling them they are useless or not good enough.

A breaking point is typically reached, and the codependent behaves in a way to gain attention. This can be where they become angry, blaming, or show other emotions they have been bottling up. The narcissist will act pleased and try to "fix" this behavior by giving extra attention and gifts to the codependent. If the codependent doesn't return to how they were originally, the narcissist may return to this behavior again.

There are many different types of codependency, but they all fall into one of these categories:

1. Physical abuse – This is the most <u>obvious</u> type of abuse and can include hitting, punching, pushing or shoving. If your partner has been physically abusive to you, you may need to seek help in the form of a shelter or support groups.

2. Emotional abuse – This is the most <u>common</u> type of abuse. Emotional abuse can include name-calling or insults, threats, constant criticism, making fun of someone's appearance or telling them they are worthless or stupid.

3. Sexual abuse – This is any type of unwanted sexual contact or behavior. Sexual abuse can involve threats, coercion, or taking

advantage of someone sexually when they are unable to give consent, for example due to the influence of alcohol or drugs.

4. Mental abuse – This involves degrading and insulting a person in a non-physical way. It can include making threats to harm you or your reputation, as well as stalking, harassment, invading privacy and manipulating by controlling money and other resources.

5. Neglect – This is when a person intentionally does not meet your emotional needs.

Codependents who were abused growing up tend to find partners who are the same type as their biological family. The child of an alcoholic person, for example, may end up with a partner who is also an alcoholic. They may stay in these relationships because they don't realize they have the power to change them or they deserve better. People with codependent behaviors can also feel responsible for a parent staying sober when he or she drinks too much.

6. Self-harm – This is most common in people with Borderline Personality Disorder and involves deliberate self-injury, such as cutting, burning or hitting.

7. Food and eating disorders – People who are codependent may feel they don't deserve to eat a healthy diet or they are unworthy of having good things in life. They may use food or starvation as a way to punish themselves for past behaviors and to try to control their lives.

8. Alcohol and drug abuse – People who are codependent may end up abusing alcohol or drugs to mask their feelings, avoid their problems, and cope with stress.

9. Poor self-image – A common result of being in a relationship with a narcissist is that the codependent feels worthless or like a failure. They might feel ashamed of themselves, for example, if they have been sexually abused and don't report it.

Codependents usually build relationships with people who also have codependent tendencies or other mental health issues, including substance use disorders. This is because codependents do not typically feel satisfied in healthy relationships. Abuse in these relationships typically cycles because the codependent returns to the relationship due to feelings of guilt for leaving and worry about being alone.

Other forms of this behavior may include enabling someone's addiction, taking responsibility for someone else's actions and feelings, or staying in an abusive relationship to avoid abandonment. It is important to recognize your own codependent behavior so you can change it. You can get help for codependency by getting involved in a support group or finding an individual therapist. Any type of therapy will be beneficial if you bring yourself to take the first step and go to your first therapy session, then following through with continued treatment to help change your life forever.

Many people have suffered from childhood trauma and are now living in the adult world with a different worldview than most. They don't know how to cope with their emotions or how to share their power, feelings, and thoughts. This can be very difficult for them; it may mean they will take on more responsibilities than they need to and keep details of their lives secret so no one can hurt them or control them.

It is important to remember that you're not alone in your feelings and experiences. Many people feel the same way as you do. If you feel codependency is a problem, it is important to recognize it and work with your feelings to solve your problems so you no longer feel that others need to fix them. This will be a very difficult process, and you need support from others to get through it.

Notes

_____

_____

_____

_____

_____

_____

_____

_____

_____

Chapter 4:
Codependents and Their Personalities

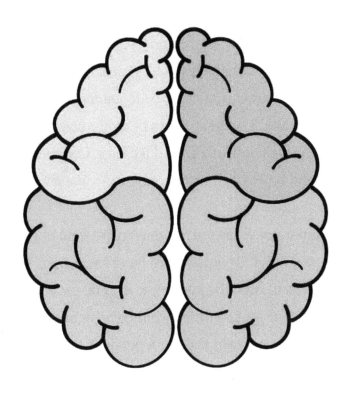

C odependents often have specific personality traits that influence or even dictate how the recovery process will proceed. These individual traits may become the reasons why codependents struggle and resist recovery. Family members and the loved ones of codependents often feel hurt, disappointed, frustrated, and/or angry. These are understandable feelings usually linked to how codependents deal with emotional situations.

The personality characteristics of codependents are also called codependency traits. These traits can be generalized into three areas: behaviors, ways of thinking and feelings. Codependents usually have several types of dysfunctional traits in each of the three areas of codependency.

Codependent personalities are not new to the field of psychology, nor are they old news. Because there have been many codependent relationships in modern history, it is to be expected that different codependent personalities would evolve and arise as time passed. It is also important that codependent traits and personalities be treated on their own because each trait can influence recovery in a different way.

It is an inexact science to determine whether the codependent has a personality disorder or not. Personality disorders are often characterized by long-standing patterns of perceiving and relating to the world, others, and oneself. Codependency doesn't have a specific definition, but it does have traits that codependents might display. As I describe in this book, codependents have several different types of personality traits that they display, and these traits could be classified as personality disorders.

Some personality traits and characteristics of codependents include:

- Denial: Codependents tend to be very good at denial. They deny the presence of a problem, even when they are in the middle of it. Many times they are aware that there is a problem, but they don't want to admit it exists because they are afraid to face the consequences of change.
Codependents also deny their own feelings and emotions, both positive and negative. Codependents will deny the fact that they have a problem by saying something like, "I'm okay, you are the one with the problem." They will also deny their feelings by saying things like, "I'm fine, I don't need to talk about it." Codependents may also deny their emotions and feelings by drinking, drugging, or even staying busy to avoid thinking about them.
- Blame: Codependents tend to blame others for everything that goes wrong in their lives. They are very good at finding fault with others. They also tend to have an external locus of control, believing they are the product of outside circumstances and other people. They feel as though whatever happens in their lives is not a direct result of their own actions.

- Distorted thinking: Codependent thinking is distorted by projection, denial, blame, and minimization. Codependents tend to project their feelings onto others by assuming others feel the same way they do about a situation or event. They deny their own feelings and assume others are denying theirs as well. Codependents tend to blame others for things that go wrong because they don't want to admit they are wrong. They also minimize their own mistakes and behavior and exaggerate the actions of others or the seriousness of a situation.

- Compulsive helping: Many codependents have a compulsive need to help people. This need to help is so strong that a codependent will often neglect their own needs to meet the needs of others. Compulsive helping is a way for codependents to prove to themselves and others that they are good and worthy people.

- Preoccupation with other people's affairs: Many codependents have an intense interest in other people's problems. They feel compelled to solve their friends' and family's problems, even when they are not welcome or wanted. Codependents will offer advice, listen to problems, help solve a problem and even fix things for other people. Many codependents derive their own sense of self-worth by "helping" others solve their problems.

- Possible low self-esteem: Many codependents have low self-esteem. They usually see themselves as worthless, defective or flawed. Many times they don't see anything good about themselves at all. They may also be ashamed of themselves or their past behaviors. Codependents may even see themselves as victims of a bigger problem or set of circumstances.

- Problems with boundaries: Codependents tend to have difficulties with boundaries, both internally and externally. They struggle with knowing where they stop and someone else begins. Many codependents have difficulty saying "no" to other people, especially if it means the other person will be upset or disappointed. They have problems setting healthy boundaries with others, and they feel guilty when they do. Codependents also struggle with knowing what their own needs are. They often have a hard time discerning between someone else's needs and their own legitimate needs.

- Passive-aggressive behavior: Many codependents display passive-aggressive behavior but many times without even recognizing it. They resentful and hold grudges against certain people but never confront the person or deal with the problem directly. They will often criticize and try to control the behavior of the other person indirectly. They also have a habit of being very critical of others, but they rarely, if ever, offer praise or support.

- Problems with trust: Many codependents have problems with trust because they often can't distinguish between trustworthy people and untrustworthy ones. Codependents will sometimes go out of their way to help someone who has caused them harm in the past. This often includes long term abusers, such as ex-partners. Codependents tend to give everyone the benefit of the doubt and rarely, if ever, have realistic expectations of others.

- Abandonment issues: Many codependents struggle with abandonment issues because they either experienced a parent or caregiver abandoning them in childhood or they fear they will be abandoned themselves. They can either cling desperately to their loved ones out of fear or they can push people away, fearing rejection. Many codependents have an extremely difficult time letting go of a relationship that is unhealthy, bad for them or over. They often feel guilty for doing so.

- Problematic sexual behavior: The sex lives of many codependents are in disarray. Many codependents have addictive sexual behaviors that interfere with their lives and cause problems in relationships and friendships. They often have a very hard time saying "no" to sex. They tend to engage in high-risk sexual behaviors, often placing themselves and others in dangerous situations. Many codependents struggle with infidelity, compulsive promiscuity, and/or compulsive masturbation.

- Excessive need to be liked: Many codependents are extremely sensitive to rejection and criticism. They tend to put other people's needs and wants before their own. They want to be liked by everyone and often go out of their way to help someone. Sometimes they are too nice, in an effort to be liked.

Codependents also have a tendency to be enablers, tolerating abusive or inappropriate behaviors because they don't want to hurt others' feelings or cause conflict.

- Disproportionate emotions: Codependents are usually highly emotionally reactive. Their emotions are often out of proportion to the situation. They tend to have problems with their moods, which can swing from one extreme to the next. They also have an exaggerated sense of guilt and shame.

- Fear of abandonment: A core fear for many codependents is that friends, family members or loved ones will abandon them or leave them. They tend to put aside their own needs and want to keep others close.

- Chronic anxiety: Many codependents suffer from severe anxiety. They fear that something terrible is going to happen and often feel as if they are losing control over the situation. Anxiety is the most common co-occurring condition suffered by those with borderline personality disorder.

- Mood swings: Many codependents experience sudden and extreme mood swings. These can be brought on by stressful events or seemingly for no reason at all.

- Guilt: Many codependents feel overwhelming guilt. They suffer from what is commonly referred to as "survivor's guilt." This is an irrational sense of guilt that you should have done something differently, even though there was nothing you could have done.

- Perfectionism: Many codependents are perfectionists. They tend to put unrealistic expectations on themselves and others. Perfectionists are often hard on themselves and others, causing them to be anxious and self-critical.
- Being caretakers: Many codependents are caretakers. They feel responsible for everyone's welfare, both at home and in the workplace. They often agree to take on more than their share of responsibility, which is not a good thing if you also have ADD because you will never be able to complete everything asked of you, and this can cause feelings of inadequacy.

If you have a feeling that you have any of these symptoms or behaviors sound familiar to you, you may be suffering from post-traumatic stress disorder due to childhood abuse. If this is the situation, you are not alone and there are treatments available that will help you to feel better. Do not suffer in silence. Reach out for help and do something positive so you can have a better quality of life.

Notes

Chapter 5:
The Habits of Codependent Individuals

C odependency is a word that has been increasingly used over the last several years. Codependents are people who depend too much on others. But what does this mean?

In many cases, codependents are people who are so desperate for approval and affection that they find it in all the wrong places and from all the wrong sources. Codependents can typically be found in co-dependent relationships or in relationships with individuals who have problems of their own.

The common habits of codependent individuals are:

1. Codependent people usually have a problem with low self-esteem. They tend to base their own self-worth on the way that other people treat them. A codependent person often feels more comfortable when they have the approval of others. They may not even notice they are seeking approval in the first place. A codependent person could be highly critical of themselves and place more value on the opinions of others.

2. Codependent people can usually be very sensitive to the moods and opinions of other people. They often walk on eggshells, feeling they have to choose their words carefully and not say anything that might upset others. A codependent person can worry about what people think about them but may try their hardest never to show this inner worry in the way they act or speak.

3. They are indecisive and easily feel overwhelmed. They may be afraid to make decisions on their own because they are fearful of

making the wrong choice. This can cause them to stop making decisions at all. For example, if a codependent person is given the choice between two activities by someone they may just go along with whatever that other person wants them to do.

4. They tend to be helpless, hopeless, and pessimistic. Because of their fears and feelings of inadequacy, they often feel powerless to overcome their problems. Rather than take action to make their lives better, they usually just sit around and wait for something to change.

5. They have a hard time saying "no". This is the case when they are given a request and it would hurt the other person's feelings not to accept or because failing to do what is asked of them would cause conflict in the relationships.

6. They often don't like themselves very much. Because they base their own self-worth on how other people see them, they may constantly be comparing themselves to other people. They are usually extremely hard on themselves. Most of the time, they never feel they are good enough.

7. They are often isolated and withdrawn from others. Sometimes, codependent people don't feel they matter at all to other people, so it would just be easier to stay away from others altogether. There are times when they prefer to be alone rather to deal with the emotions that come from being with other people.

8. They deny there is a problem in the relationship or even when they are constantly disappointed by the other person. They tend

to be very persistent and continue to make excuses for why the other person has failed to meet their expectations.

9. They find it hard to accept compliments or celebrate successes, and they don't possess an overall positive outlook on life.

10. They often have a problem with addiction. Codependent people have a tendency to turn to drugs and alcohol to fulfill a need they are unable to fulfil on their own. They use these substances as a way of escaping their problems and coping with the feelings that come from low self-esteem, approval seeking, and the lack of control over their lives. These habits tend to cause them more problems than solutions.

11. They tend to be irresponsible and untrustworthy. They are usually very sensitive to the needs of others, so they may not follow through on their promises or obligations. For example, if a codependent person is planning on doing the dishes, they may decide at the last minute to watch TV instead and just hope that someone else will take care of it. They also tend to leave messes everywhere that they go and are often late in paying their bills.

Many codependents need to know what is going on in the lives of their loved ones and want to be included in all their activities. They want to know they are still loved, even if they are not treated well by their significant others. They tend to be so desperate for approval that compromise their own self-worth and overlook a partner's problems or shortcomings.

Many codependents take it upon themselves to fix their significant others' problems and make them better people. They may attempt to move a loved one out of the "addiction" cycle or change a partner's personality. But these attempts are rarely successful and only serve to delay the inevitable.

The goal of this type of behavior is simple – codependents want to feel needed or wanted by their loved ones, and they want to believe they can help their partners become better people.

Some codependents are attracted to individuals with an "addictive" personality. They have an intense need to take care of someone and rescue them from their problem. However, these individuals don't realize that they are being used and manipulated by their loved ones.

As long as a codependent can find someone in need of help, he or she will supply the support needed for the relationship to survive. In the end, codependents are usually disappointed by their loved ones' actions. They begin to lose trust in them and may eventually become disenchanted with the relationship.

In order to avoid being codependent, it is important that you learn to value your self-worth and accept the fact that you are an individual. You should also learn to stand up for yourself in a loving way and not allow others to use or abuse you.

Notes

Chapter 6:
Codependency and Boundaries

C odependency recovery is a long and sometimes tedious journey. It's a process of undoing years of thinking, behaving, feeling, and reacting in unhealthy ways. This healing journey is about learning to take care of ourselves in an honest, loving and respectful way by setting boundaries.

It has been said that "codependents often have poor boundaries". Moderating the use of "poor" here, I agree with the sentiment. Most (not all!) of us codependents struggle to establish, maintain, and respect boundaries. We have poor boundary skills because we grew up in families without enough of them.

It was often a disorganized household, an alcoholic home, where boundaries were not clear. There were usually lots of conflict but few consequences for irresponsible behavior.

I'm talking about "unchallenged" behavior. There were no healthy consequences in our childhood homes. We kids didn't have any say in the chaos. And we couldn't defend ourselves against our parents' excessive or inappropriate behavior because we had no way to do so (i.e., consequences).

We grew up in surroundings where we were not safe. It was a house divided, when two or more family members fought each other with no resolution. The fighting just kept on going... nobody wins in a situation like this.

When our boundaries are violated repeatedly as children, they become weakened. We grow up not respecting our own limits or the limits of others.

As adults, we continue to have trouble setting boundaries and practicing self-care. We're still trying to fix broken situation. We tell ourselves that we'll be better parents if we set better boundaries. But the fact is that boundary setting is something that can be learned in time.

When our boundaries are weak, it's because of the way we were raised, not because of what we want for our children or want to become as adults. As codependents, in order to establish solid personal boundaries, it's important that we first work on strengthening our own self-esteem.

We need to learn how to self soothe, take care of ourselves, and get our needs met. It's a different journey from codependency recovery. It takes time.

Self-care is about taking responsibility for oneself and setting boundaries on the outside world. It's about recognizing the rights of others when it comes to interactions with oneself, asking for what one needs and wants in an honest way - and feeling safe enough to do so.

The first step is the hardest and that's why it's important to start with self-awareness. As we become more aware of our feelings, needs and values, we're better able to verbalize them diplomatically. This is important because people with codependency issues tend to be indirect, hard on themselves, and often passive aggressive in their interactions with others. By becoming better at self-expression, it's easier to set limits on others. Some codependents are able to do this on their own.

How to set boundaries when you're single

Some codependents choose to not get involved with others at all. They prefer to be on their own or they enter into relationships, where they set the ground rules from the outset. These boundaries are often healthy and appropriate.

Some codependents choose co-dependency in relationships and end up failing at them because they don't know how to maintain good personal boundaries within that relationship. Their boundaries are sometimes appropriate but often violated by their partner(s). Setting healthy boundaries is a learned skill. It takes time, and it's a process.

How to set boundaries with others

The first step is discovering what your feelings are with respect to the situation. Some codependents are overly defensive or don't know how to ask for what they want or need in non-threatening ways. Practice makes perfect!

They learn by doing...like most things in life. Some examples of good boundary-setting questions are: What do I feel? (e.g. anxious, angry, sad, hurt, scared...etc.)

What do I need? (e.g. understanding, reassurance, time out...) How do I want to be treated? (e.g. respectfully, kindly...)

Start by asking for what you need in small ways, see if others respect your boundaries and honor your requests. If they're willing to make some adjustments for the good of the relationship and everyone involved...great! If not, that's okay too. At least you've asked...and you've gotten feedback!

Some people are impatient with the codependency recovery process. They want to be better at setting boundaries right away. That's why I wrote a post on "How to Ask for What You Want ".

Read it and keep working on your self-care skills so you'll feel safe enough to communicate in a way that works for you.

The process definitely includes asking for what we want or need in a respectful way...so others will be more likely to give it to us. That's because others often don't know our needs or what makes us happy. If we're not emotionally healthy, it's difficult to ask for what we want or need in a way that doesn't threaten others. That's why it helps to practice setting boundaries and communicating with others until it becomes a habit. As with all things in life, repetition helps!

How to set boundaries in dating relationships

Unfortunately, many codependent people have relationship problems that stem from their inability to establish healthy boundaries.

Some people are bold and assertive (even aggressive) about what they want and need in the beginning of a relationship. They're ambitious about establishing limits early on. If the other person doesn't respect their boundaries, they call it quits...sometimes before anyone else even gets a chance.

Others are the opposite. They're too timid and shy to even mention boundaries and limits. Either way, there are some important things to remember when establishing boundaries in a dating relationship.

What's right for one person might not be right for you. All the information is not always available to you in the beginning of a relationship. You may need to spend time getting to know one another better before deciding what's best for you. What you want from a new dating partner may change over time as well...and that's okay!

Asking for what you want in a respectful way usually works better than making demands. You'll might get more of what you want if you're respectful and specific about what you need.

For example, rather than saying, "I demand we do something fun on Friday night", say something like, "I'd really like to go see (movie title) on Friday night." Then just express your feelings, needs, or concerns in a hopeful way. You might say, "I'm worried that we won't have any fun if we go to another dinner party instead of the movie."

It's okay to change your mind. If someone is persistent and won't take "no" for an answer, you do have the right to end the relationship. However, most people find it helpful to try saying, "no", in a kind way one time before making a decision. You might say, "I'm sorry, but I can't go to dinner with you this weekend. Perhaps we can do something another time."

There's nothing wrong with letting people down gently. The best relationships are strengthened by respect and open communication. There's a good chance you'll be able to work things out if the person really cares about you. But there's also a chance that this person won't stop bugging you about your boundaries. Then it might be time to let them go and find someone else.

Notice the difference between a "soft" and "hard" no. A soft no is often just a gentle way of saying no, such as, "I'm really busy this week. I wish I had time to do that with you." This type of response can still be disappointing for the other person, but it's much easier to handle than a hard no.

Any kind of forceful response can become a hard no. For instance, if you respond to a question by saying, "No, I'm not," or "No, you can't," you're responding with aggression. Similarly, if you threaten someone or become angry when they ask for something from you, that's also aggressive. A soft no is much easier to take than a hard no.

It makes sense that it will be less difficult to deal with, but it's still important to understand the differences between these responses. A soft no may be easier to take, but it's not necessarily genuine. It can be just as much a defense mechanism as a hard no and can be even more frustrating for the person delivering the response.

Verbal Defense Mechanisms

Defense mechanisms are conscious or unconscious reactions to feelings or situations that are uncomfortable for us. They help us to avoid situations that make us feel anxious or stressed out in some way and allow us to avoid our emotions.

Verbal defense mechanisms include things like sarcasm or white lies. They sometimes include responding with behaviors such as defensive anger or withdrawal. These reactions are often useful, even necessary, when we're feeling threatened. When in a situation where we feel personally attacked, we can sometimes respond best by not responding at all.

Rarely do people set out to be deliberately hurtful or dishonest. It's more common that people with codependency react with sarcasm because they have difficulty dealing with their own feelings and emotions.

Some of us over-react to situations and say things we later regret because we haven't learned how to express our emotions or talk about them in a healthy way.

When someone asks you a question, it's okay to preface your answer with, "I feel. . ." or "In my opinion. . ." That way, you're not being dishonest...you're just stating your honest feelings at the time you're answering the question.

Sometimes it's okay to be evasive. For example, if you don't want to answer a personal question, you can say something like, "I don't feel comfortable talking about that," or "That's not something I really want to get into right now."

In the long-term, it's better to answer questions honestly instead of being evasive. Honesty is the best policy! Harmful verbal defense mechanisms include lying (less commonly) and denying your own feelings (more frequently).

These types of responses can be particularly harmful in relationships because they're less likely to be obvious. They're harder to identify and deal with.

Denying your own feelings allows you to avoid dealing with your own emotions and the situation at hand. But it can cause you to feel like you're constantly walking on eggshells, trying to predict how the other person will react or what they might think if you say what you feel.

It allows the other person to control your emotions and responses and ultimately control you. Denying your emotions also make you feel like you're not good enough and that you're constantly disappointing or letting someone down.

In relationships, it's important to be genuine and honest at all costs. Codependents are often hard on themselves and try to be perfect in an effort to please others. However, people with codependency issues often can't see how their behaviors affect the people around them, and they usually don't mean to offend or hurt someone when they do something wrong.

Notes

Chapter 7:
Improving Your Co-Dependent Life

The first thing you can do to improve your life is to learn everything you can about codependency. You may have been codependent for many years before you realized it and reading about codependency and the behaviors that go with it can be a real eye-opener. Discovering that you are codependent can be very painful, but it is the first step toward improving your life. Once you have discovered that you have codependent trait, and a pattern of dysfunctional codependent behavior patterns, you can begin to learn and grow from this knowledge.

Codependency is an addiction to other people's approval, and you are the enabler. You feel a compulsion to be there for others when they need you because you get a high from being needed and wanted. You also get a rush when you are able to fix someone else's problems or make things go right for them. If the thrill of being needed and wanted is reduced or stopped, you will begin looking for another person who needs your help. You may also begin to feel anxious and depressed because when you are needed and wanted, your self-esteem rises.

Codependency is a learned conduct transmitted from parent to child. If you grew up with a kind of parent or parents who were dysfunctional in one way or another, you are more likely to become codependent yourself. But if you didn't have dysfunctional parents, you can still learn the codependent behaviors from your friends or other people you interact with.

If you are codependent, then you will also be an enabler. You enable others to continue their dysfunctional behavior because you believe that if they don't get their way or get attention from you, they would suffer greatly. You have spent your life enabling co-dependent behavior in others and have made it your job to fix other people's problems. Enabling is the opposite of helping someone learn how to solve their own problems by themselves.

How to improve your co-dependent Life?

To improve your life, the first thing you need to do is to detach emotionally from other people. This is the hardest thing for a codependent person to do because they have been codependent all of their lives. Codependents get their identity and self-esteem from being needed and wanted. Take a deeper and hard look at the relationships you have. Are you in a relationship with some-one who is emotionally, physically, financially and/or psycholog-ically abusive to you? If so, then get out of the relationship now. You will never be able to fix the other person, and you can't change another person no matter how much you love them. You can only change yourself.

If you are still in this relationship after repeated attempts to make things better for yourself and your partner, realize that this is what life looks like on this planet as a codependent. You will for-ever be at the mercy of other people's moods and problems. Once you accept this and decide to change your life, you can begin im-proving your life. Stop enabling others' behavior because you are not helping them by giving into their demands and rescuing them from their problems.

Let them learn the hard way that their problems are their own responsibility and don't bail them out or make things right for them if they fail to fix things. You will only be making yourself sick in the process. Look at all of the relationships in your life. Are these relationships healthy and mutual? Are you getting your needs met in the relationship, or are you giving more than you are receiving?

If it is a one-way relationship where you are giving and giving, and not getting what you need, then end it now. You can't get anything back until you first give whatever it is to them. This is the time to look at the way your family functions as well.

Are you in a codependent relationship with someone in your family? Is there an enabler in your family who has enabled dysfunctional behavior for many years? If so, you can't say for sure that you won't follow in their footsteps. Improve your own personal health.

Start eating right and exercise regularly to become healthier. Drink plenty of water and get at least seven hours of sleep each night to improve the quality of your life and reduce stress. Find a hobby or something you are passionate about and make time in your schedule to do it at least once a week. Find something that helps you get in touch with your spiritual self if you have one. Accept the codependent behaviors you have lived with all of your life and begin to change them immediately. Let go of any guilt or shame inside about being codependent. You can't control how you were raised, nor can you control what other people do to manipulate or take advantage of your life.

The only thing you must control is yourself, and it starts with taking responsibility for your own actions. Stop blaming others for your past codependent behaviors. When you are ready to make changes in your life, set realistic goals to achieve these changes. For example, if you want to reduce your weight, don't say that you are going to lose 100 lbs. by the end of the year.

You will fail if you set yourself up for failure. Instead, make small changes in your lifestyle each week until you reach your goal weight. If you want to create a better relationship with your spouse or significant other, start talking to them about how they can change their behavior and show more love and respect for you.

Take Responsibility for Your Actions

If you have been blaming others for the way they have treated you in the past, or if you have been blaming yourself, now is the time to stop all that. You may feel shame about some of the things you did in your life, but don't be ashamed. Blame nobody for the things you have done to others or the things that others have done to you. Take responsibility for your own actions, and it will set you free.

Live Your Life Today

You only get one chance so make it count! Codependency is a learned behavior, and if you were raised in an environment where codependency was all around, chances are you are a codependent person today. It is not so much about blame as it is about taking responsibility for your own life.

Stop blaming other people for the way you feel inside. Today is a new day; it is your opportunity to make things right with the world around you. Parents who are codependent tend to project their own issues onto their children so they can justify their own behavior. This leads to a confused child who doesn't know what they should believe or how they should act in the world. Don't be that child. You only have a chance at life, so why spend it as some sort of victim?

You are not a Victim!

Stop feeling sorry for yourself. It's not attractive nor helpful. Feeling sorry for yourself is simply another form of blaming others for the way you feel. Think about your life today - do you really want to continue living this way? Do you want to keep feeling afraid, guilty and ashamed? Really think about this question, even if the answer may be painful initially. You deserve to be happy. You deserve to feel joy in your life. You deserve to have a life that makes you proud of who you are and what you have accomplished. It is up to you to make it happen - nobody else can do it for you.

How to Stop Being Codependent Victim

Here are some ideas to stop being a codependent victim:

1)   Stop blaming other people for your feelings and your life experiences. You choose how you respond to other people and your life experiences. This is the bottom line. You choose whether you are going to be a victim or are going to take back control of your life and feel proud of who you are.

2)   Stop thinking that other people have power over your thoughts, feelings, and emotions. Your own thoughts and feelings have power over you - not the thoughts and feelings of others. Start taking responsibility for your own feelings and stop blaming others for your circumstances in life. It's all about taking responsibility for what happened in your past.

The past has an influence over your present and future. Maybe not 100%, but it is a lot stronger than you think. And oftentimes, the way we were raised causes all sorts of difficulties when we enter adulthood. It's important to realize these influences from our past and take responsibility for them so we can move.

3)   Stop trying to fix other people. Do not take responsibility for other people's problems, issues, or circumstances. It is not your job to fix others' stuff or rescue them. Let go of your need to be needed and focus on what you want in life instead. You may be surprised by the positive side effects that come from this change in thinking.

4)   Stop being afraid of making healthy changes to improve

your life situation. You cannot be happy and content in life until you are willing to make healthy changes. You can change the way things are for you now by making the decision to change on your own. You are the only one who can make the decision, and only you have control over healthy changes.

5)   Stop being a people pleaser. Everyone is a people pleaser to some extent, but if that is all you do in life, it is not a good thing at all. People pleasers have low self-esteem and lack confidence in many areas of their life. They give too much and expect too little in return. Start saying "no" more often when people are asking you to do something because you don't always have to say, "yes", just because someone else wants you to.

6)   Stop thinking that others have it better than you. We all have our own issue. It's not so much about how bad your situation is, but, instead, how good you will feel when you decide to change your life for the better.

7)   Stop going behind other people's backs about them. Talking behind another person's back is a passive aggressive form of communication that says a lot more than words ever could. It is very important to know how to communicate directly with the people you love and care about so there is never a need for to talk behind their backs.

8)   Stop being jealous of others. Jealousy is the fear of not having what someone else has or being what someone else is. Jealousy comes from comparison, and oftentimes, we compare ourselves to others on purpose to make ourselves feel better. When

you make a choice to stop comparing yourself to others, then you will feel less jealousy. You will also notice that other people are not thinking about you as much as you think they are.

9) Stop saying "yes" when you want to say "no". Learning how to say "no" is an important part of taking control of your life. You cannot change the way things are in life until you learn how to say "no" and stand up for what you believe in. When you want to say "no" and then make yourself do something you really don't want to do, it is called "covert aggression"; it's a sneaky way of trying to control the outcome of a situation. Stop being sneaky and manipulative in your interactions with other people and, instead, start choosing to be honest and open in your communication.

If you take responsibility for your own life, you will feel good about who you are and what you have accomplished. You will enjoy peace of mind knowing that anyone who has been involved in your life is not going to affect the way you live it anymore. Take responsibility for your own actions as well as how you feel on the inside. You are the only person who can change the way things are. It is not so much about blaming other people anymore as it is about taking responsibility for yourself. You can begin to change your life and the way you respond to others.

Notes

Chapter 8:
Changing a Codependent Relationship

C odependence is born of the difficulty to accept and be one-self. It's also a response to being in an environment that doesn't support one's own sense of self. There isn't anything wrong with seeking connection with others, but codependent relationships are not about connection; they're about control. The intense need to control is driven by an underlying shame and fear regarding who one is and how one fits into the world. It comes from the idea that if you can control your partner, you can feel safe in the world.

The emotional energy fueling codependent relationships is rooted in fear, shame and obligation. It's the belief that your needs and desires don't matter; rather, you are here to meet someone else's needs. What's often misunderstood about codependency is that it doesn't just occur in romantic or family relationships. It can exist within friendships, work settings – even with strangers.

Codependency is not about love; it's about control. The drive to control is always fueled by fear, shame and obligation. In a codependent relationship, you are so connected to the other person that you actually become your partner. You feel what they have felt and experience their emotions as though yours. It's not about caring; it's about losing yourself in another person.

Codependents often see themselves as "fixers" because they're always trying to find solutions for other people's problems or issues. In actuality, they're not fixing anything; they're just enabling their partner's illness or problem to continue.

Codependents don't have their own solutions. They don't know how to support themselves, so they go into the relationship thinking, "If I can just figure out how to make it work, then my problems will go away." Their underlying issues wrap around and become a part of the other person's. The codependent doesn't have solutions for themselves; instead, the focus is on others.

Codependent relationships are usually not about romance: they're about control and fear. Codependents aren't interested in intimacy but in protection – from being abandoned or hurt, or from feeling alone.

These connections are not based on love or mutual interests; rather, they're based on fear and obligation. The reason you feel so dependent on the other person is because you believe that your survival depends on them. Being alone feels like death to a codependent person, so the only way to feel safe is to control someone else's behavior.

When the codependent person learns how to love themselves, they learn how to set healthy boundaries. In this new place of independence, they'll be able to tell the other person what they need and refuse to be manipulated.

A codependent person doesn't have to lose their whole relationship to become independent. Instead, they can take an active role in the relationship by making a conscious choice as to where their energy goes. They can stop giving and start focusing on how they want their lives and relationships to look and feel.

For many people, being codependent is a way of life. Codependency causes them to be emotionally dependent on others, but not just in romantic relationships. Friends, family and co-workers are the common people who can trigger codependency issues in someone else.

Codependents often gain a lot of self-worth from their roles in these relationships. When they're cared for by someone else, the codependent person feels valued and loved. This is what makes it so difficult for them to leave a relationship that's not working out. The codependent person doesn't feel whole without someone to take care of them. If they're being manipulated or mistreated, the lack of self-worth will be that more apparent.

The world tells everyone to love themselves and stand up for themselves, but when it comes to codependency – it's different. Codependents don't know how to have healthy self-esteem because they are so focused on their interactions with other people. They may believe they are unworthy of being loved. Rather than standing up for themselves and leaving a horrible relationship, they continue to stay in the relationship because that is what they believe is best.

The way codependency manifests itself varies from person to person. It isn't always obvious to the people around the codependent person either. Codependent people tend to be very passionate about other people; sometimes it looks over concern about how others are feeling or behaving. They can be preoccupied with other people's problems, and sometimes, they get so absorbed into what someone else is feeling that they neglect their own feelings and needs.

Codependent people often put too much pressure on themselves to take care of everyone all the time. It becomes overwhelming. They hope others will see how great they are by being so kind and putting their needs aside for others.

The thing about codependency is that it isn't a character flaw or something like that. It's an issue of self-worth. People tend to feel bad about themselves for what they are doing. They don't know how to set boundaries and learn how to take care of themselves.

Couples often experience codependency because they both have low self-worth or are afraid of failing or being rejected if they stand up for themselves or leave the relationship.

If a couple has a codependent relationship, it may appear that the non-codependent person is not as nice as he or she seems. In actuality, the codependent person has low self-worth and may be trying to get someone else's attention or approval. It's usually more what is going on internally than how that person behaves toward others. The codependent needs love and approval from the other person to feel good about themselves.

Codependency in relationships is a pattern that goes back to what each person had learned in childhood. It's not just about the family environment, but also how each person was parented. Codependent people often didn't have healthy role models growing up. They may have had a parent or caregiver who was needy, controlling, or manipulative. They may also be dealing with an issue from their past – like an abuse situation, emotional problems that made them feel fearful or unworthy of being loved. Sometimes, they were abandoned by a parent. All these things may lead a person to think that it's normal to be codependent.

In the end, codependents are those who suffer in their relationships. They are trying to make up for it by being close to someone else and focusing on them instead of themselves. However, what they really need is someone else to love and accept them for who they are – not as someone they can fix or help.

For you to change the codependent relationship, you have to change the underlying beliefs and emotional energy that drive it. Shame-based emotions like fear, anger, guilt and resentment fuel the controlling elements relationships and make you feel like you are stuck in a loop. To become more of yourself and begin to change the dynamics of your codependent relationships, you must do three things:

1. Learn to accept who you are today.
2. Practice setting boundaries.
3. Develop self-compassion and self-love.

Accept Who you are Today

Accepting who you are today is not always easy because it requires accepting all parts of yourself, including those you don't like or even despise. When you've been struggling with shame for years, it's easy to see your flaws and shortcomings as insurmountable. This can keep you from self-acceptance. Meditation is a powerful tool that helps clear your mind; it will allow you to get in touch with yourself and become aware of what's truly holding you back from happiness. You may discover that your fears are not rooted in reality or that something specific in your life is causing them (a past relationship, childhood trauma, etc.).

Changing Codependent Relationships

Changing codependent relationships requires addressing the underlying issues that created them in the first place. It's not enough to detach from your partner; you must also learn how to attach to yourself and accept all of who you are today. Only then can you start to make positive changes.

In order to detach from a codependent relationship, follow these steps:

1. Identify what makes you feel healthy and happy. There are many things that will do it. For example, if you like to eat healthy food, work on eating healthy food. If you find that it is hard to focus with someone in the room, focus on what makes you feel happy and healthy when they are not there.

2. Get help from people who believe in your potential. Surround yourself with individuals who value your potential and love you for who you are instead of what they want you to be.

3. Know what you want. Avoid getting into a relationship until you have spent some time thinking about who you are.

4. Avoid people who are bad for you. Part of your recovery from codependency will be learning to avoid people who do not care about your well-being.

5. Practice self-care: be kind and say nice things to yourself. When you are kind and loving with yourself, you will be able to attract people into your life who feel the same way toward you. Understand that healthy love is not about sacrificing yourself; itis not about giving yourself p for someone else.

6. Focus on your own life while letting go of your partner's life choices. When you are in a codependent relationship, your life and your partner's life are intertwined. You may feel that your life is dependent upon what happens in their life.

7. Develop your own solutions for your life. Avoid trying to fix your partner and, instead, develop your own solutions.

8. Slow down and give yourself time to detach. You cannot detach from a codependent relationship in just a few days or weeks. Detaching from a codependent relationship takes time. Avoid acting impulsively when you are emotionally unstable or feeling jealousy.

9. Develop a support system outside of the relationship with people you can trust, who will love you and support you no matter what happens in your romantic relationships.

Setting Boundaries

Codependency is all about controlling your environment; therefore, stop trying to control the people in it to have healthier relationships.

Follow these steps:

1. Start defining what makes you feel good about yourself and what doesn't work for you anymore.

2. Focus on your needs and wants.

3. Express your feelings in a respectful, non-judgmental way.

4. Learn how to set boundaries with people who are emotionally abusive and don't respect you.

Developing Self-Compassion and Self-Love

Begin the process of self-acceptance today by working on three essential things: learn to be compassionate with yourself, practice self-love and detach from negative relationships (even if they're family members or close friends.

If you're having trouble accepting yourself because you feel as though your life is a failure, remember this: no one can define what success is for you except you.

You cannot live anyone else's life. The only person who has the authority to decide whether or not you are successful is YOU. You get to decide how well your life is going, and that definition doesn't have to be rooted in money. Instead, it can be based on things like health, relationships and happiness.

If you accept all parts of yourself, you'll be able to build a life –
and a loving relationship – based on the virtues that matter most
to you. This is the key to changing codependent relationships and
reclaiming your power and individuality.

Notes

_____

_____

_____

_____

_____

_____

_____

_____

_____

_____

_____

_____

_____

_____

_____

_____

Chapter 9:
Common Misconceptions
About Codependency

There are many misconceptions about codependency that prevent people from seeing that they are hurt and need help. Here are some common misconceptions that people believe about themselves, their codependent relationships, and the treatment of co-dependence:

1. Codependency is a personality disorder

A personality disorder is a disorder that manifests in four main areas: pervasive thinking patterns, affectivity, interaction in relationships and impulse control. Personality disorders are chronic, long-standing psychological patterns that can be severe enough to cause distress or impairment in social and occupational functioning.

The characteristics of codependency-oriented people have little in common with disruptive personality disorders. In fact, they are different in many ways, including the ability to form healthy relationships. According to the Diagnostic and Statistical Manual of Mental Disorders (DSM-IV) a personality disorder is diagnosed by these criteria: 1) an enduring pattern of inner experience and behavior that deviates markedly from the expectations of the individual's culture; 2) it is inflexible and pervasive across a broad range of personal and social situations; 3) it leads to clinically significant distress or impairment in social, occupational, or other important areas of functioning.

2. Codependency is the same as codependency

Codependency is a relationship with an addiction; it's a relationship between an addict and a non-addict who has bonded with the addict and often has doubts about their own identity, their own personal value, and fears abandonment by the addicted person. Codependency is not a personality disorder. Codependency is an addiction to another person, who has an addiction. It is about mutual dependency, not about feeding off of each other's dysfunctionality. It is a codependency, not a codependency.

3. Codependency makes people do things they don't want to do

This myth suggests that people with addictions and other dysfunctional behaviors have no choice in their behaviors or recovery process and that they are compelled by some outside force to remain sick or continue their destructive behaviors. This is not true. People who have addictions continue to engage in addictive behaviors out of choice, even when it serves no purpose and produces no positive results.

4. Codependency is caused by an unhappy childhood

People with codependency issues did not have an unhappy childhood; they did not grow up in a dysfunctional family or were abused during their childhood. They are addicts and their co-dependent partner is addicted to them as well.

5. It's easy to walk away from an addictive person

The real causes of codependency are complex and not well understood. A combination of biological, psychological and social factors contribute to the development of codependency and its symptoms. It is also clear that co-dependent behavior occurs in emotionally and physically healthy people, who have been well supported and well-loved in childhood. It is true that they have a fear of abandonment, but this is not a result of an unhappy childhood.

6. Codependency is not treatable

Research has proven otherwise. The majority of people who have come to recovery for codependency and seek help from reputable sources find recovery and lead healthy, happy lives. Much like other addictions, treatment for codependency typically begins with detoxification.

7. Only women get co-dependent

Co-dependent behavior is not gendered. Both women and men can be either co-dependent or addicted. (Women, on the other hand, are often co-dependent.)

8. Codependency is as serious problem as the addicted person's addiction

Codependency is not a disorder. It is a symptom of an underlying disorder, most commonly an addiction, and often other disorders such as depression, anxiety and panic disorder. Codependency often stems from fear and low self-esteem, making it hard for people to fulfill their own needs and develop healthy relationships that do not center around tending to the needs of others.

9. Codependency is something you're born with

Codependency is not inherited or passed on from one generation to the next. It is a learned behavior that develops over time, often during early adolescence. As a result of being raised by overprotective, controlling parents or caregivers, children learn to sacrifice their own needs for the needs of others. It also develops when a child is raised in a home with multiple problems such as addiction, mental illness, abuse or violence.

10. A co-dependent person and their partner must have separate treatment

There are many benefits of individual and couples therapy done at the same time, although most treatment centers do not offer this service. In individual counseling, addicts learn to carry the message of recovery back into a relationship that is very much in need of healing and recovery, while they continue with their own recovery program. Couple's counseling allows both partners to discuss the detailed events of their lives and relationship together. Individual recovery is essential to the success of a relationship.

11. Co-dependent people are weak, needy and helpless

Co-dependent people tend to be very loyal and protective of their loved ones as well as very tolerant and forgiving. This can lead them to tolerate a great deal of pain and injustice without ever confronting their addicted loved one. There is nothing weak or helpless about this, especially when you consider that they are often sacrificing their own needs and wants to take care of someone incapable of caring for themselves completely.

12. Codependency is a result of poor parenting

Bad parenting can lead to feelings of low self-esteem in children, but it does not create codependency. Parents who are abusive or overprotective may inadvertently contribute to the development of codependency, but they do not cause it.

13. The only treatment for codependency is counseling and group support meetings

Many treatment centers offer individual counseling and group support sessions as a means of beginning the recovery process. Many also offer 12-step programs such as Al-Anon or CoDA (Co-

Dependents Anonymous). However, individual counseling can be costly and more difficult to obtain on an ongoing basis. Support groups for co-dependents can be very helpful because they offer a safe place to go where members understand what you are going through and offer support when you need it the most.

14. There is one cause of codependency

There are lots of reasons for the development of codependency, including psychological and biological factors. Most often, a combination of circumstances leads to the development of codependency, including a dysfunctional family system. The best approach to treatment is through counseling and support groups designed specifically for co-dependent individuals.

15. A person with codependency cannot change the other person or change what is happening in their relationship with an addicted loved one

While the addicted person may need to get into treatment in order to change, you can take steps toward recovery and healing by yourself. You can change your own thoughts and actions and learn new ways of coping. In addition, you can create a strong support network that will make you feel more secure and confident to deal with any challenges in the future.

16. The relationships of co-dependent people are always difficult, painful, abusive or troubled

While some people with codependency may experience difficult, abusive, or troubled relationships, not all co-dependents do. For example, a person may have married someone who is not an addict and has had a healthy relationship throughout his or her life. Others are in healthy relationships but tend to be codependent in other important areas.

17. A co-dependent cannot love honestly and deeply

The love and concern of a person with codependency is not fake or shallow. Their need to be in a relationship is real, and their capacity for deep intimacy is true and intense. It may simply be that they are overly dependent on a relationship for their self-worth. They may have been born into a situation where they learned that their value was dependent upon taking care of someone else's needs.

Co-dependent love may be more conditional than that of an addict. An addict's "love" is conditional on being loved back and taking care of his or her needs. The co-dependent's "love" is conditional on making the person he or she loves happy.

18. A co-dependent does not know how to please himself

He or she will do almost anything for the person he or she loves, even if it hurts him.

19. Codependency is caused by low self-esteem

The core characteristics of codependency include anxiety and fear of abandonment, experiences of shame and humiliation, self-sacrifice, and an inability to be truthful and direct with others, resulting in feelings of inadequacy and feelings of being transparent or invisible. This is not the same as having low self-esteem.

20. A co-dependent believes that he or she will always be judged

This is a tell-tale sign of a co-dependent. Co-dependents are constantly afraid of being judged, which makes them seek approval from others at all times.

21. A co-dependent will go out of his way to help a person in need without thinking much about his own needs and desires

This misconception about codependency creates a lot of pain and misunderstanding for people who are suffering in their relationships with addicts and their children. It's important to understand that every human being is not born dependent. We did not come into this world addicted; codependency develops as we grow up and has many causes that are difficult to understand. But we can learn about the origins of codependency, the effects it has on addicts and their loved ones, how it can be overcome, and what treatment options are available.

How can these misconceptions be changed? Here are some ways you can correct some of the negative myths about codependency:

Seek support. There are many sources of information about code-pendency and recovery available to help you understand what you are going through. Seek out support groups in your area and try to find a counselor or therapist with some experience in working with co-dependents, even if it means traveling a bit farther. Just being yourself with others who have similar experiences can be very helpful. You deserve to be happy and healthy, and a support group can help you learn what you need to know to begin your journey toward recovery.

Talk about it. Codependents are often afraid to talk about what's going on because they fear that others will judge them as weak or needy. Nothing could be further from the truth. The sooner you start, the sooner you'll become healthy and happy. The longer you keep your feelings inside, the harder it will be and the longer it will take to recover. You deserve better than that, and so do your loved ones.

Learn how to change your thoughts. Whether you've had some therapy or not, it's important to learn about how thoughts create feelings. When you feel bad, you likely have a negative thought about yourself or others. Learn how to change that thought into a positive one. Changing your thoughts is not easy for codependents because it can be difficult to get started without someone else helping you, but there is hope and help for you.

Learn how to express yourself honestly and directly. It can be particularly hard to do this if you've been told that you are too sensitive or too needy. But by learning how to express yourself honestly, you'll be able to gain more respect for yourself and have healthier relationships with others.

Notes

_____

_____

_____

_____

_____

_____

_____

_____

_____

_____

_____

_____

Chapter 10:
More Tips and Advice for Overcoming Codependency

C odependency is a condition that exists in people who need to be needed. They have an excessive or unhealthy need for attention, approval and acceptance. They are dependent on the acceptance of others and are distressed when they do not receive it. If you have unhealthy or excessive love towards someone linked with fear, guilt or shame, it may be a sign that you are codependent. The individual may have had traumatic life experiences, leading to the development of a codependent personality.

There are ways to overcome codependency. It is important for you to understand that you have the power to change if you want to change. You should not continue in a relationship that makes you feel miserable. Improve your self-esteem so your self-image becomes positive and realistic. Do not compare yourself with others or what you have achieved in life. Your achievements are your own and you should be proud of them. If you are not happy on your own, learn to enjoy time alone.

Being dependent on others for the rest of your life is not a healthy way to live. You should not take on a responsibility beyond your abilities or that you are not prepared to handle. You should let go of the tendency to please everyone else at all times. This will get you into trouble from time to time. You should try to live your own life and not be concerned about what others think of your lifestyle and personal choices. However, you may need help in overcoming codependency if it is a severe problem that has been with you for a long time. Help can be obtained from various mental health professionals who are trained in this area.

You need to become aware of your own feelings and those of others around you. This will enable you to interact with others without hurting them or yourself. Cultivate empathy for others by taking the time to listen and understand their feelings and emotions. This will enable you to relate to them on an emotional level. If your relationship with another is not working, you should try and work out the situation so it becomes healthy and positive for both. You do not have the right to interfere in the lives of others just because you feel they need your help.

Your friends and family are there for a purpose and not every situation needs you as an intercessor or solution provider. You should be there to help them in times of need and not feel that you have the job of giving their life meaning. Accept the fact that some people do not want your help and learn to accept it.

Learn how to say "no" when someone asks for your help, assistance or advice. If you do not think you can give them a positive answer, it is better to say so. Stop trying to change or save everyone you meet even if you think they are in a bad situation.

Let them have the space and time to learn and grow. Do not interfere or give them unsolicited advice even when you feel you know what is best for them. Give the people around you the space to be themselves without judging them. You should not try to change people just to make yourself feel better.

You should surround yourself with people who do not have problems as this will help improve your own self-esteem. Poor quality friendships do not improve your life, but they can destroy it; this is a fact that codependent people need to understand.

You should also be prepared for a relationship that is not like what you read in romance novels or see in movies. A healthy relationship will not hurt nor leave scars on you emotionally. A healthy relationship will help you become a better person and enhance your self-esteem by being supportive of your partner and yourself.

Stop searching for a knight in shining armour. You should not expect your partner to solve your problems and make you happy. Understand that being dependent on someone else makes you weak and vulnerable. Remember that one day, you will be on your own in this world.

You need to accept and love yourself before you can be accepted by others or can accept them in your life. You need to know that you are a good person and not what your codependent traits say about you. You should learn to say "no" when others ask for too much of you. You should learn to trust yourself so when other people let you down, you will know how to pick yourself up again and continue with your life.

You must also learn to love yourself and become aware that you are an important part of this world. There is good in everyone so know that you are not lacking in anything. Even though you have a lot of codependent traits, you can change them if you are willing to work at breaking free from them.

Learning to overcome codependency is a slow process that takes some time; there will be setbacks along the way. Do not give up trying to overcome codependency in your life. Take each day as it comes and learn from your mistakes. You will find that life is a lot easier when you move on and let go of the past.

No one is perfect. You can change and learn to be happy and free. So make the decision right now to let go of codependency in your life. Are you willing to work at a positive change in your life?

The first step in overcoming codependency is simply deciding that you want to become free from it. This may seem an easy thing to do; but for many, codependency runs deep and can take some time to overcome. Just knowing that you have a problem can be the first step.

Do not depend on others for your happiness. If you are codependent, there is a good chance that you depend on others for your happiness and self-worth. If you can let go of this need, you are on the path to overcoming codependency in your life. No one else can make you happy because happiness comes from within and not from other people. If your happiness relies on how others make you feel, your self-esteem will be based solely on the opinions others have of you.

Notes

Chapter 11:
How to Build Self-esteem

M ost people involved in dysfunctional relationships have low self-esteem. People who have high self-esteem can also be codependent. They have a false self-image or a low tolerance for discomfort. All of us, at some time, will fall into that category. When we are in a state of denial about behaviors, we engage in what is not good for us and keep repeating those behaviors; it is time to ask ourselves if we are codependent.

Before we can begin to change ourselves, we have to change our beliefs. Let me repeat myself. You do not need other people's acceptance or approval to feel good about yourself. To feel good about yourself and develop healthy self-esteem, you have to believe you deserve love, respect, and kindness from others; but they are not responsible for your self-worth or self-esteem.

Beliefs that codependents need to work on changing:

1. I need other people to like me.
2. I must be needed by other people to feel worthwhile or valid.
3. I have to do things for other people to feel worthy or loved.
4. My self-worth is dependent on the needs of others, not on my own true feelings, desires and needs.

Codependents often struggle with these types of beliefs:

1. I must be perfect and have everything together to feel good about myself.

2. I have to be perceived as being better than, or equal to, other people to feel worthy.

3. I must give more than I get for it not to be a one-sided relationship.

Codependents struggle with self-esteem because they are not seeing themselves clearly and accurately due to the false self they are presenting to the world, believing that is who they are. They do not see their worthiness or know how to make themselves feel good about themselves. They are not comfortable within themselves; therefore, they create outside circumstances to feel good about themselves, but this never works. They believe that they are unlovable.

We all need to find ways to feel good about ourselves, and we need to find a way to do it that does not involve being dependent on something or someone else for our feelings of worthiness. We need to become independent.

Here are some suggestions that can help you develop healthy self-esteem, no matter what problems or obstacles you are facing:

1. How you treat yourself is in direct proportion to how you feel about yourself and your self-worth. The way you speak to yourself is a gauge of your self-esteem. The way you say things to yourself and the language you use are a clue as to how you feel about yourself. Use encouraging and positive phrases and speak to yourself in warm, affirming ways.

You would never use cruel or degrading language on some-one else. Be kind, gentle and considerate of yourself when no one else is around.

2. Set goals for yourself that are realistic and based on your own needs, desires and abilities. Take time to set short- and long-term goals for yourself. Break them down into steps if needed and celebrate your successes.

3. Get to know yourself better by journaling or talking to a trusted friend or therapist. Ask yourself what you want in life. What is important to you? What are your deepest feelings and thoughts? What do you personally value most?

4. Have realistic expectations about what you can accomplish in a certain period of time, or this year or this month. Be gentle with yourself and make goals that are attainable.

5. Start small when trying to make changes in your life. Make one change at a time and work on it until it sticks. Then, move on to the next issue.

6. Stop using other people to fill the voids or holes in yourself that need to be filled by you from within, not from some-one else's behavior or acts, such as a gift, trophy, a win, an achievement, their love for you, etc.

7. Be kind to yourself. You don't have to torture yourself when things do not go the way you wanted. Use self-love and kindness and be gentle with yourself. You'd be amazed how your life will be easier as a result. And how much stronger you will feel about yourself.

These are suggestions for codependents to work on. You need to be aware of what is going on inside of you in order to change. You need to be aware of your feelings, needs, and wants. You need to become aware of the language you use and the way you think about yourself. Use your feelings to guide you. If you feel sad or angry, and it feels like it is coming from something you are doing or not doing, then stop and listen to what your feelings are telling you.

It is important that you listen to yourself first and not look for someone else's approval. You do not need someone else's approval in order to feel good about yourself. If you don't think that you can change on your own, get help from friends or family members who care about you, a counselor or therapist, or join a support group for codependents to work with others going through the same issues.

Notes

Conclusion

C odependency is actually not a disease; it's a pattern of learned behavior. After you read this book, if you feel you have codependent traits, please do not become discouraged. The most important step is to acknowledge the problem and then try to change it.

As with any other negative habit, it takes time and a lot of effort. But with practice, you can unlearn any negative behavior. And that is the key to recovery – unlearning the patterns of codependency.

A codependent may have trouble acknowledging their own feelings and needs because they've spent their whole life thinking about someone else. This means that they may not be able to express how they really feel. Instead of talking about themselves, they try to change the subject in an attempt to make sure that other people are okay and taken care of.

If you do not feel like you have control over your behavior or if there is something about yourself that makes you feel bad, therapy may be in order. The process can help you examine the past so you can decide where you want to go in the future. Do not let codependency define your life; instead learn to define yourself.

Codependency is a term for a type of dysfunctional helping relationship that results from an insecure and dependent personality where one person's well-being is dependent upon another's dysfunction. The co-dependent person has a tendency to ignore their own needs, often resulting in adverse effects on the helper's personal life.

Codependency is a problem that many people suffer from but few people speak about. It can be very difficult to understand, and even more difficult to overcome. The first step is admitting that you have a problem. The second step is learning more about it. Try to increase your awareness every day until you reach a point where you are conscious of the way you are currently acting. Then try to change it.

It may be hard, but don't give up because it is so important. This will help you realize something about yourself that allows you to make further discoveries later. Maybe you can't do it as quickly as you think, but you can do it so don't give up.

Always keep in mind that there are persons out there who love you. Many of them are trying to help you in any way they can. Please get help if you need it but try to do it yourself first if at all possible. Think about what this book has tried to teach you and start applying it as soon as possible. A day without change is a day wasted.

You were born with three innate gifts: free will, a conscience, and unconditional love.

This book has been written to help you. If it helps you, please tell someone else who may find it helpful as well.

Notes